C000001000

SPIRIT OF

DARTMOOR PONIES

THE DARTMOOR PONY SOCIETY

First published in Great Britain in 2009

Copyright text and photographs © 2009 Dartmoor Pony Society

British Library Cataloguing-in-Publication Data
A CIP record for this title is available from the British Library

ISBN 978 1 906887 23 0

PiXZ Books
Halsgrove House, Ryelands Industrial Estate,
Bagley Road, Wellington, Somerset TA21 9PZ
Tel: 01823 653777
Fax: 01823 216796
email: sales@halsgrove.com

An imprint of Halstar Ltd, part of the Halsgrove group of companies
Information on all Halsgrove titles is available at: www.halsgrove.com

Printed and bound by Grafiche Flaminia, Italy

Introduction

THE DARTMOOR PONY

The origins of the Dartmoor Pony are lost in the very mists of Dartmoor that they have inhabited for hundreds of years. The earliest mention of the Dartmoor Pony was in 1052 in the will of Saxon Bishop Aelford of Crediton. There is also another mention in 1296 when a charge was made for grazing ponies on the Moor.

The Dartmoor Pony is a small hardy breed, tough enough to stand the extreme weather of Dartmoor, which is a wild upland made up of moor, forest and granite-topped tors rising to over 2,000ft above sea level, and it receives the full force of the Atlantic gales.

Over the years the ponies have been used for many purposes. During the tin mining era they carried the tin from the mines to the Stannary towns on the edge of Dartmoor. When the mines closed they were left to roam free, apart from those required to work on the farms. This was mainly shepherding, for which they were well suited with their sureness of foot and understanding of the terrain. They also proved to be excellent driving ponies taking the family to church, market and other outings.

In 1898 the National Pony Society set up a local committee to produce a breed standard, and to inspect the ponies for entry into the new Stud Book. Except for the height, the original description of the Dartmoor Pony is almost identical to the present day breed standard. In 1924 the Dartmoor Pony Society was founded and the maximum height for a pony of 12.2h.h. was fixed at that time.

The Dartmoor Pony has a very kind nature, and with its exceptional temperament makes it an ideal pony for children. With its good build, limb and bone it can easily accommodate a small adult. With their careful movement and kind temperament they are ideal as a schoolmaster for the novice child. However they also adapt themselves to more advanced work and are used extensively for all Pony Club activities for Lead Rein, Open Ridden, Dressage, Working Hunter Pony events, hunting and driving.

In 1988 a scheme was devised by the Duchy of Cornwall and the Dartmoor Pony Society with the support of the Dartmoor National Park to safeguard the gene pool and to improve the quality of the ponies on the Moor. Approved mares, offered by the Moorland farmers from their pony herds, are inspected and taken off the open Moor during the breeding season. They are placed in enclosed areas known as Newtakes, and run with a Registered stallion from May to the beginning of October. Each Newtake has approximately fifteen mares. The resulting foals are inspected and the fillies returned to the Newtakes as three year olds. Since the scheme began several hundred foals have been born, and the first fully registered filly foal was entered into the main Stud Book in 1994.

The Dartmoor Pony is officially recognized as a Rare Breed by the Rare Breeds Survival Trust. A lot of work is done to safeguard this lovely native breed. By the very fact that its beauty and temperament make it one of the most sort after children's ponies today, it also very much helps itself, and is equally at home under the spotlight at the Horse of the Year Show, or in the mists of Dartmoor that it has inhabited for hundreds of years.

List of contributors to this book
(In Alphabetical Order)

Mr M. Ball
Mr A. Brewington
Mr. R. Brown
Mrs. V. Brown
Mrs. D. Coaker
Mrs J. Green
Mr D. Howarth-Podesta
Mr J. Jordan
Mrs D. Marshall
The Hon. Mrs M. Vanstone
Miss H. Wort-Browne

Among the rocks.

A relaxing snooze.

A Dartmoor herd.

Amongst the thistles.

Anyone at home?

At ease.

Every year in September the ponies are rounded up and moved from the higher Moor for winter grazing and shelter. This event is called 'the drift'.

Coming in on the drift.

Corralled.

Awaiting inspection at the annual drift.

Browsing . . .

A winter scene.

That's cold!

Follow me!

Coming.

Dartmoor stallion.

Cross country.

Champion mare.

Dartmoor mares.

Dartmoor ponies.

Extended family.

Dartmoors at play.

Did you call?

Follow me mum.

Foal.

Four in a row.

Above:
Black and white.

Right:
Fun in the pond.

Going . . .

. . . going . . .

. . . gone!

Having a drink.

Grazing.

Herding up at the annual drift.

Above:
Head rest.

Right:
I'm grey.

I think it's going to rain.

Home time.

Dartmoors in history. Hurricane – first furlong, Huccaby Tor Races, 1911.

The Royal Box, Huccaby Tor Races, 1911.

Is this my best side?

Above:
Where is Mum?

Right:
I'm here.

Just born.

It's time for tea.

Musical ride.

Look at me!

Moorland grazing.

Above:
Newtake ponies.

Right:
Three's a crowd.

Oh for a good roll.

Oooo – that's nice.

Round up at
the annual drift.

49

Summertime.

Reflections.

Snuggle.

Taking shelter.

Tasty.

The herd.

The moor.

This way everyone.

Peek-a-boo.

Up we go!

Water splash.

Flying!

Whispers.

You called?

Who invited you for supper?